P9-BJV-036

FAST FACT MATH

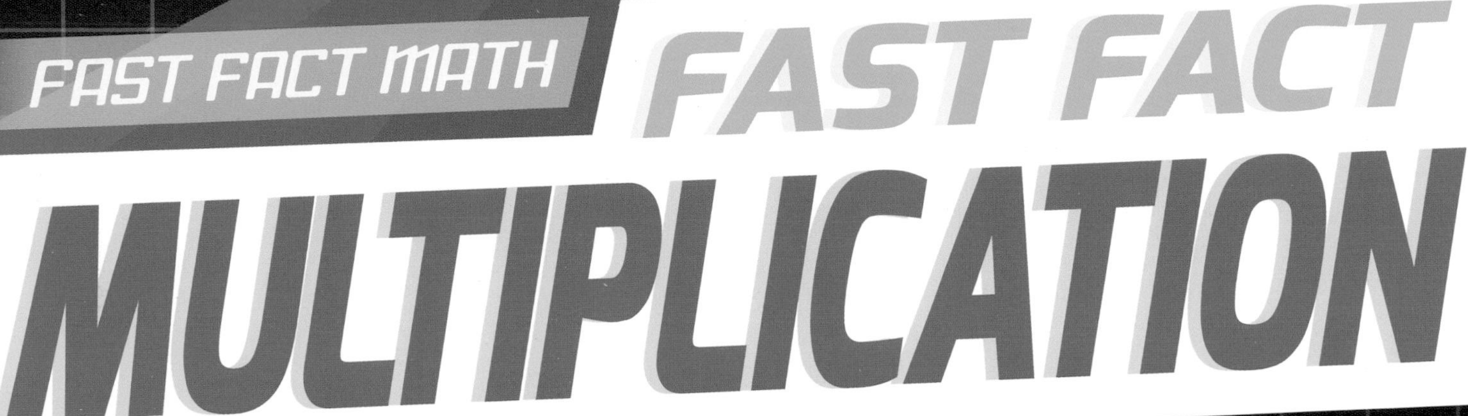

FAST FACT MULTIPLICATION

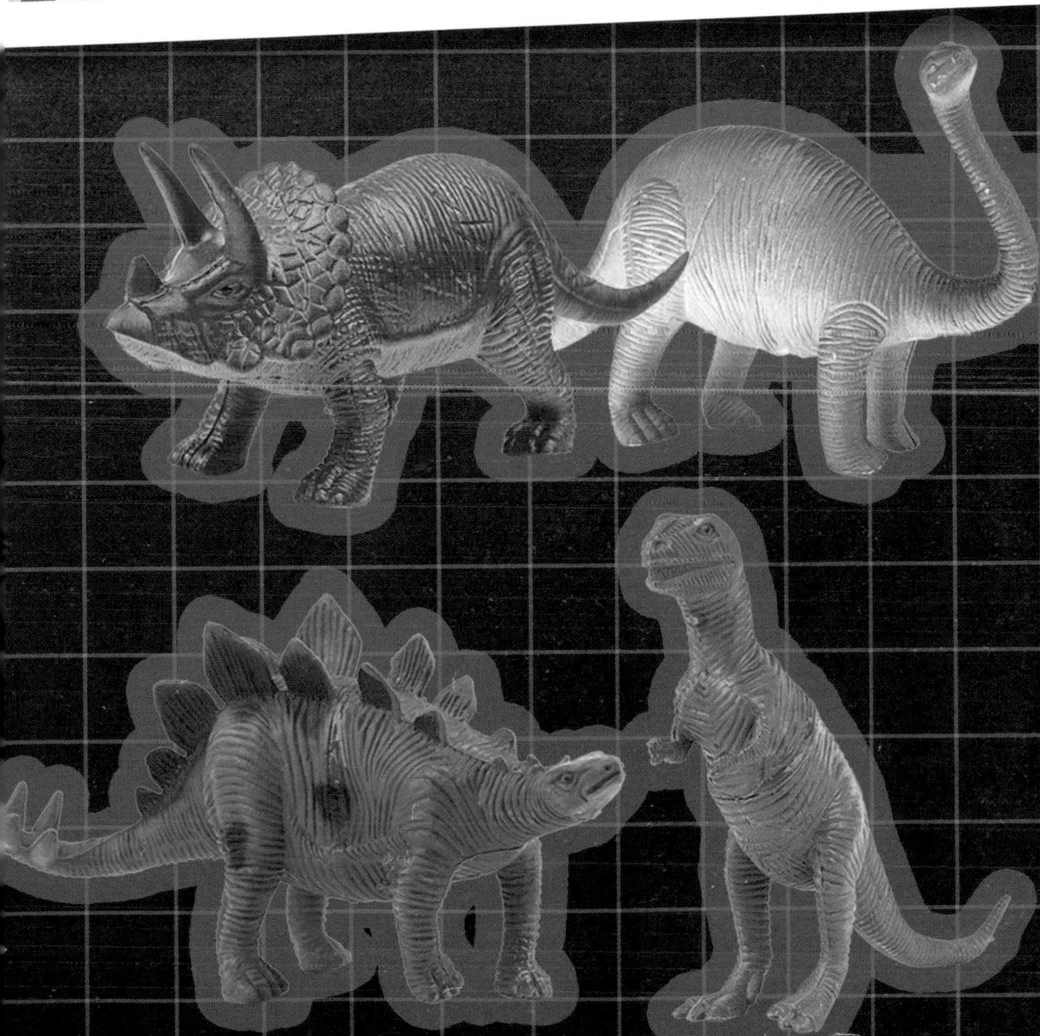

2 GROUPS OF 2 DINOSAURS

2 × 2 = 4 TOTAL DINOSAURS

BY BLANCHE ROESSER

Gareth Stevens PUBLISHING

Please visit our website, www.garethstevens.com. For a free color catalog of all our high-quality books, call toll free 1-800-542-2595 or fax 1-877-542-2596.

Library of Congress Cataloging-in-Publication Data

Names: Roesser, Blanche, author.
Title: Fast fact multiplication / Blanche Roesser.
Other titles: Multiplication
Description: New York : Gareth Stevens Publishing, [2019] | Series: Fast fact math | Includes index.
Identifiers: LCCN 2017040797| ISBN 9781538219874 (library bound) | ISBN 9781538219898 (pbk.) | ISBN 9781538219904 (6 pack)
Subjects: LCSH: Multiplication–Juvenile literature. | Arithmetic–Juvenile literature.
Classification: LCC QA115 .R6727 2019 | DDC 513.2/13–dc23 LC record available at https://lccn.loc.gov/2017040797

First Edition

Published in 2019 by
Gareth Stevens Publishing
111 East 14th Street, Suite 349
New York, NY 10003

Designer: Sarah Liddell
Editor: Therese Shea

Photo credits: Cover, pp. 1, 7 Sergiy Kuzmin/Shutterstock.com; chalkboard background used throughout mexrix/Shutterstock.com; p. 5 Dmitri Ma/Shutterstock.com; p. 8 HomeStudio/Shutterstock.com; p. 9 Alex Staroseltsev/Shutterstock.com; p. 11 (sand) Ozerov Alexander/Shutterstock.com; p. 11 (shells) Here Asia/Shutterstock.com; p. 13 David A. Ross/Shutterstock.com; p. 15 Bokeh Art Studio/Shutterstock.com; p. 17 MANDY GODBEHEAR/Shutterstock.com; p. 18 Gelpi/Shutterstock.com; p. 21 Monkey Business Images/Shutterstock.com.

Printed in the United States of America

CPSIA compliance information: Batch #CS18GS: For further information contact Gareth Stevens, New York, New York at 1-800-542-2595.

CONTENTS

Words in the glossary appear in **bold** type the first time they are used in the text.

WHY MULTIPLY?

Did you know that multiplication can make your life easier? It's true! It's a kind of math shortcut. Instead of counting by ones or adding many times, you can use a multiplication **equation** to figure out a problem quickly.

Sometimes, it's easiest to picture objects when you're multiplying so you can understand how this math **operation** works. But soon, you'll know multiplication facts by heart. This book will help you reach that goal faster. Let's get multiplying!

MATH MANIA!

As you read this book, you'll become a master multiplier. Get ready to use your math skills. Look for the upside-down answers to check your work. Good luck!

AN ARRAY IS AN ARRANGEMENT OF OBJECTS OR PICTURES IN **COLUMNS** AND ROWS. THIS ARRAY HAS 4 COLUMNS AND 4 ROWS. IT COULD **REPRESENT** THE EQUATION 4 X 4 = 16.

ADDITION MADE SIMPLE

FAST FACT: Multiplication is a way of adding numbers together quickly.

Imagine you had 6 groups of 3 dinosaurs. You need to find out how many you have in all. You could add 3 to itself 6 times. In other words, you could **solve** a long addition problem:

$$3 + 3 + 3 + 3 + 3 + 3 = ?$$

But it's much easier to write a multiplication problem that represents the same idea:

$$3 \times 6 = ?$$

Both problems equal 18. You have 18 dinosaurs in all!

CREATING ARRAYS OR PICTURING OBJECTS IN YOUR MIND LIKE THIS CAN HELP YOU UNDERSTAND WHAT A MULTIPLICATION EQUATION MEANS.

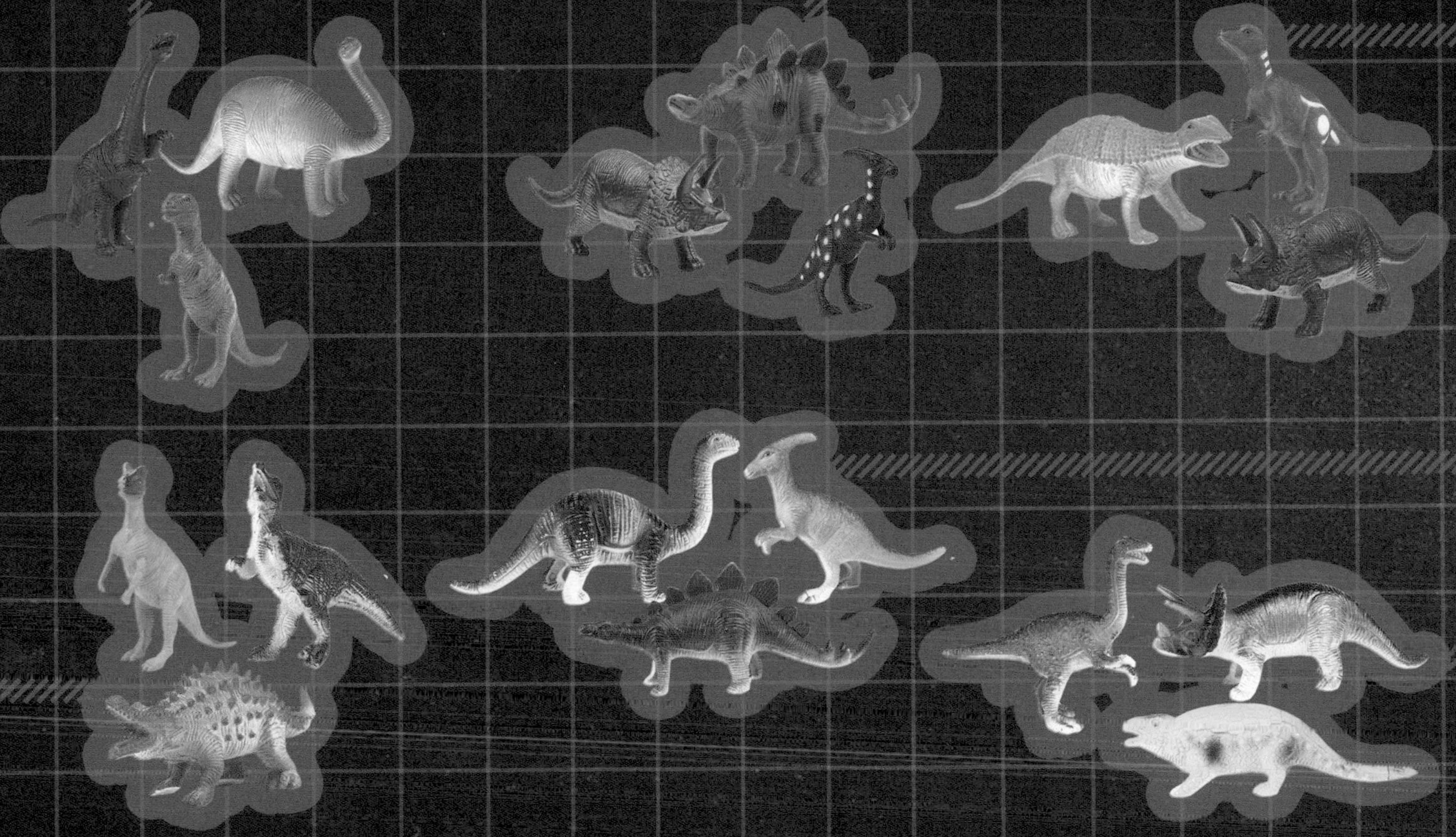

MATH MANIA!

Imagine you had a party and 8 friends came. Each friend brought 3 balloons. Solve the addition problem below to find out how many balloons there were in all. Then, solve the multiplication problem, which represents the same idea.

$$3 + 3 + 3 + 3 + 3 + 3 + 3 + 3 = ?$$

$$3 \times 8 = ?$$

Answer: 24 balloons, 24 balloons

MULTIPLICATION WORDS

Numbers in multiplication equations have special names.

FAST FACT: In a multiplication equation, the numbers that are being multiplied are called factors. The answer is called the product.

FACTORS → 2 x 3 = 6 ← PRODUCT

Here's an array of model airplanes that shows you how this equation could be represented:

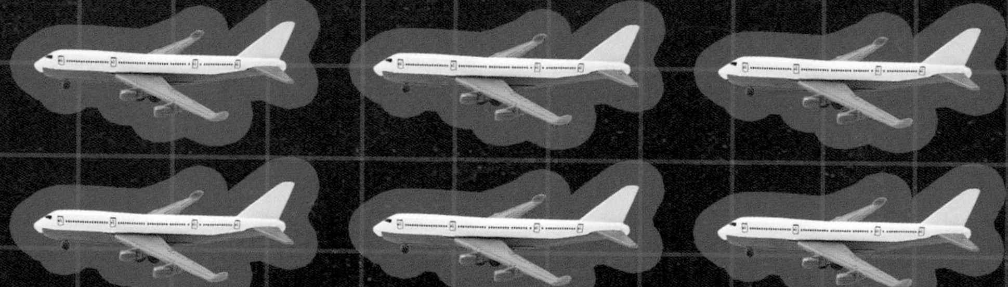

To figure out the total number of model planes, you could count each one, add the two rows, add the three columns, or just multiply 2 and 3.

AS FACTORS GROW LARGER, MULTIPLICATION IS THE EASIEST METHOD TO FIGURE OUT THE NUMBER OF OBJECTS—OR BUGS!—IN AN ARRAY.

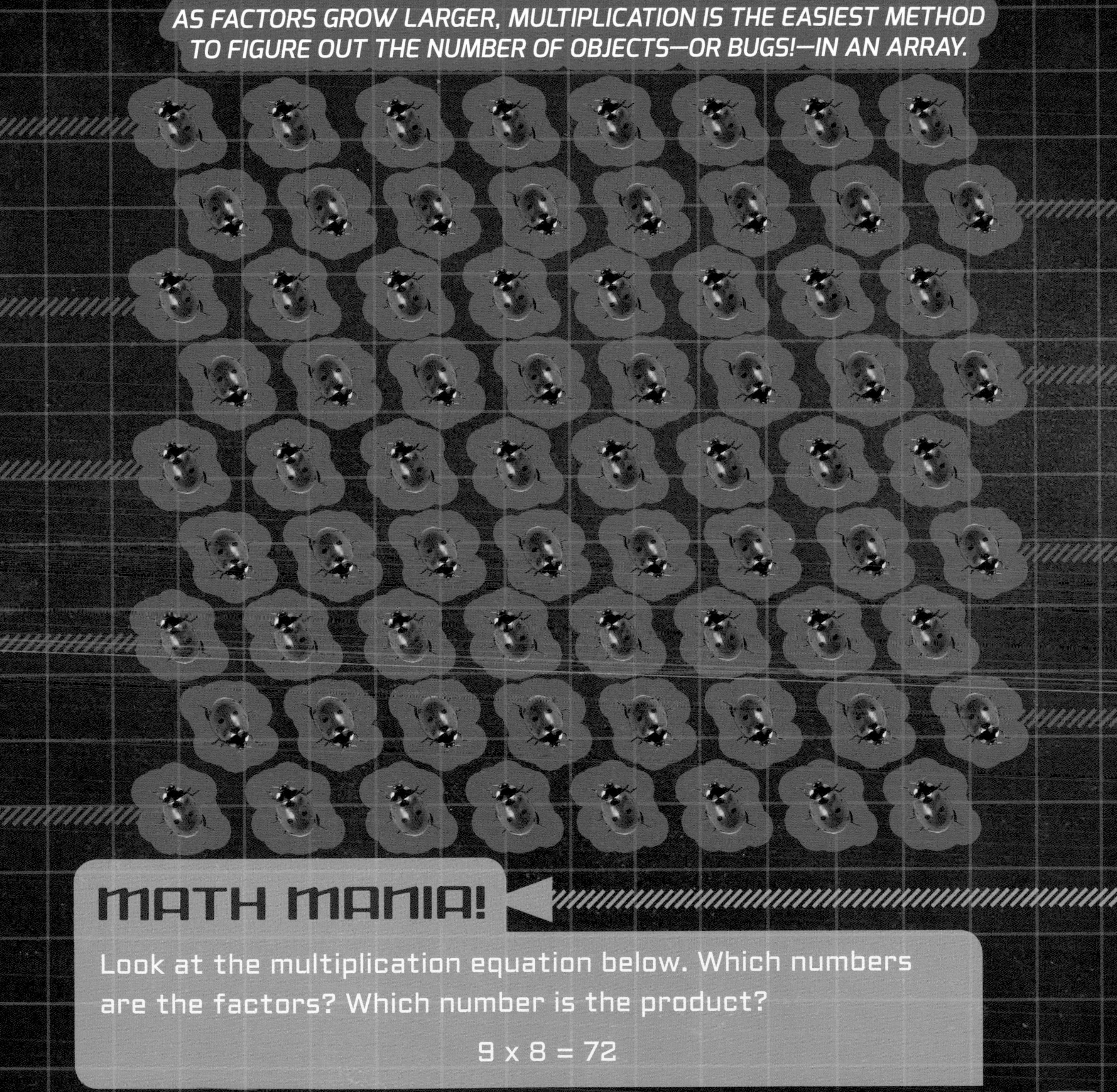

MATH MANIA!

Look at the multiplication equation below. Which numbers are the factors? Which number is the product?

$$9 \times 8 = 72$$

Answer: 9 and 8 are the factors, 72 is the product

SWITCH THE FACTORS

FAST FACT: When the order of the factors in a multiplication equation changes, the product doesn't change.

Here's an example:

$$3 \times 4 = 12$$

$$4 \times 3 = 12$$

The order of the factors 4 and 3 switched, but the product remains 12. This is called the commutative **property** of multiplication. It can be applied to any multiplication equation. That means if you know one multiplication fact by heart, you actually know two. Just switch the factors!

MATH MANIA!

Solve the problems below. Use the photos and the commutative property of multiplication to help you.

$4 \times 2 = ?$

$2 \times 4 = ?$

Answer: $4 \times 2 = 8$, $2 \times 4 = 8$

IT DOESN'T MATTER HOW YOU ARRANGE THESE ARRAYS—OR SET UP THE EQUATION—THE PRODUCT IS THE SAME!

ONE ANSWER

FAST FACT: If you multiply any number by 1, the product is the original number.

This is called the identity property of multiplication. You can represent this math rule with the equation:

$$n \times 1 = n$$

Replace n with any number and the product will be equal to the same number. Here are examples:

$$7 \times 1 = 7$$

$$52 \times 1 = 52$$

$$100 \times 1 = 100$$

Think about how these equations would be set up as an array. There would only be 1 column or 1 row of objects.

THERE'S 1 ROW OF 7 STAMPS. THIS COULD REPRESENT THE EQUATION 1 X 7 = 7 OR 7 X 1 = 7.

MATH MANIA!

Use the identity property of multiplication to fill in the missing numbers in the equations below:

a. 28 x ? = 28
b. 67 x 1 = ?
c. ? x 1 = 98

Answer: a. 1, b. 67, c. 98

THREE FACTORS

FAST FACT: When three or more factors are multiplied, the product is the same no matter which factors are multiplied first.

This fast fact is called the associative property of multiplication. Let's try it:

$$3 \times 5 \times 2 = ?$$

The fast fact tells you that it doesn't matter which two numbers you multiply first. Let's use **parentheses** to show our choice:

$(3 \times 5) \times 2 = ?$	OR	$3 \times (5 \times 2) = ?$
$15 \times 2 = 30$		$3 \times 10 = 30$

The product is 30 either way!

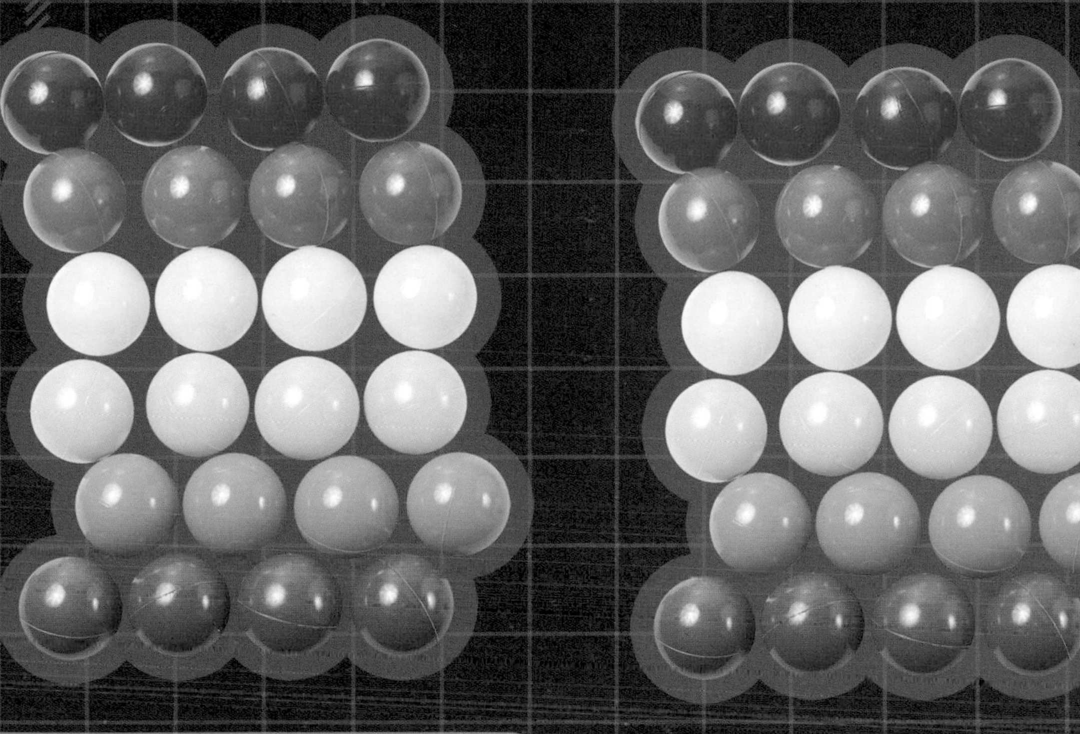

MATH MANIA!

Think about the associative property of multiplication as you solve the word problem below. The photos on this page may help.

Kim and Tim are collecting balls to make a ball pit. Kim places her balls in 6 rows of 4 balls each. Tim does the same thing. How many balls do they have in all?

6 x 4 x 2 = ?

Answer: 48 balls

A FASCINATING FACT

FAST FACT: The sum of two numbers times a third number is equal to the sum of each number times the third number.

This fast fact is called the distributive property. For the problem below, it means you can add the numbers in parentheses and multiply the sum by 8:

$$8 \times (5 + 2) = ?$$

$$8 \times 7 = 56$$

It also means you can multiply each number in the parentheses by 8 and then add the products:

$$8 \times (5 + 2) = ?$$

$$(8 \times 5) + (8 \times 2) = ?$$

$$40 + 16 = 56$$

Both methods equal 56.

Think about the distributive property as you solve the word problem below. Try solving it using both methods as shown on the opposite page. Which do you prefer?

> Four friends decided to earn money by washing a neighbor's car. They each earned $6 for washing the car. Then, they each got a $2 tip. How much money did the friends earn in all?

$$4 \times (\$6 + \$2) = ?$$

Answer: $32

THE DISTRIBUTIVE PROPERTY GIVES YOU A CHOICE ABOUT HOW TO SOLVE A PROBLEM!

A TABLE TOOL

FAST FACT: A multiplication table is helpful for practicing multiplication facts.

Look at the table on the next page. The numbers on the left side and the top are factors. The number in the square where the row and column meet is the product. Use the table to find the product of this equation:

$$9 \times 9 = ?$$

Put your finger on the number 9 on the left side. Now, put your other finger on the 9 on top. The row and column should meet at the square that says "81."

MULTIPLICATION TABLES ARE FUN WAYS TO PRACTICE MEMORIZING MULTIPLICATION FACTS.

x	0	1	2	3	4	5	6	7	8	9	10
0	0	0	0	0	0	0	0	0	0	0	0
1	0	1	2	3	4	5	6	7	8	9	10
2	0	2	4	6	8	10	12	14	16	18	20
3	0	3	6	9	12	15	18	21	24	27	30
4	0	4	8	12	16	20	24	28	32	36	40
5	0	5	10	15	20	25	30	35	40	45	50
6	0	6	12	18	24	30	36	42	48	54	60
7	0	7	14	21	28	35	42	49	56	63	70
8	0	8	16	24	32	40	48	56	64	72	80
9	0	9	18	27	36	45	54	63	72	81	90
10	0	10	20	30	40	50	60	70	80	90	100

MATH MANIA!

Use the multiplication table to answer the questions below:

a. When you multiply an odd number by an even number, is the product odd or even?

b. When you multiply an odd number by an odd number, is the product odd or even?

Answer: a. even, b. odd

MULTIPLYING INTO THE FUTURE

Did you know that doctors multiply? They might need their patients to take **medicine** many times each day. That means they'll need to multiply the amount of medicine by the number of days to know how much to give them.

Every **career** requires multiplication. You'll want to know how much you'll be paid per hour. Multiply that by the number of hours you worked and you'll know how much money you can expect. Don't leave the multiplication to someone else. Math is a powerful tool. Use it!

MATH MANIA!

Review the properties of multiplication. Match each equation on the left to the property on the right.

a. 10 x (3 + 2) = (10 x 3) + (10 x 2)

b. 32 x 1 = 32

c. 9 x 6 = 6 x 9

d. 4 x (7 x 8) = (4 x 7) x 8

1. associative property of multiplication
2. commutative property of multiplication
3. identity property of multiplication
4. distributive property

Answer: a. 4, b. 3, c. 2, d. 1

THE MORE YOU PRACTICE MULTIPLICATION PROBLEMS, THE FASTER YOU'LL ANSWER THEM—IN YOUR HEAD!

GLOSSARY

career: a job that someone does for a long time

column: a group of things written or arranged one under another

equation: a statement in math that two values are equal

medicine: something that is used in treating illness or easing pain and that is usually in the form of a pill or a liquid

operation: a mathematical process (such as addition or multiplication) that is used for getting one number or set of numbers from others according to a rule

parenthesis: one of a pair of marks ( ) that are used around a word, phrase, sentence, or set of numbers. Its plural form is "parentheses."

property: a special feature of something

represent: to stand for

solve: to find the correct answer for

FOR MORE INFORMATION

BOOKS

Arias, Lisa. *Multiplication Meltdown*. North Mankato, MN: Rourke Educational Media, 2015.

Becker, Ann. *Multiplication*. New York, NY: Crabtree Publishing, 2010.

Wingard-Nelson, Rebecca. *Division and Multiplication: It's Easy*. Berkeley Heights, NJ : Enslow Publishers, 2014.

WEBSITES

Multiplication Facts
www.mathplayground.com/multiplication01.html
Practice your multiplication facts.

Properties of Multiplication
www.ixl.com/math/grade-3/properties-of-multiplication
Quiz yourself about the properties.

Publisher's note to educators and parents: Our editors have carefully reviewed these websites to ensure that they are suitable for students. Many websites change frequently, however, and we cannot guarantee that a site's future contents will continue to meet our high standards of quality and educational value. Be advised that students should be closely supervised whenever they access the internet.

INDEX